K
Is for Krishna

Written and illustrated by Pratibha Sarkar, PhD

K Is for Krishna

Written and illustrated by Pratibha Sarkar, PhD.

Edited by Samita Sarkar, Hons BA (cum laude).

Acknowledgements

The following books from the Vedabase website (https://www.vedabase.com/en/books) were used in the preparation of *K Is for Krishna*:

Bhagavad Gītā As It Is

Śrīmad Bhāgavatam (Bhāgavata Purāṇa)

Śrī Caitanya Caritāmṛta

Teachings of Queen Kuntī

Transcendental Teachings of Prahlāda Mahārāja

I thank my dear daughter, Samita, for her help in realizing a dream I have had since she was a little girl. I wished to write a children's book that I could read to her, but now that she has grown up, she has helped me to publish this book through her imprint and with her encouragement.

I hope that you will enjoy sharing this book with your child.

Dedication

To my spiritual master and all the pure devotees.

This book is prepared for parents and children to read together.

May you always keep Krishna in the center of your life.

The Bhagavad Gita 18:46–48

"By worship of the Lord, who is the source of all beings and who is all-pervading, a man can attain perfection through performing his own work.

"It is better to engage in one's own occupation, even though one may perform it imperfectly, than to accept another's occupation and perform it perfectly. Duties prescribed according to one's nature are never affected by sinful reactions.

"Every endeavor is covered by some fault, just as fire is covered by smoke. Therefore one should not give up the work born of his nature, O son of Kuntī, even if such work is full of fault."

A is for

Arati

Prayers offered to Krishna

We offer to Krishna water, flowers, light, incense, and we ring the bell, symbolizing all the senses (taste, smell, sight, touch, sound).

BG 4:27

"Others, who are interested in self-realization through control of the mind and senses, offer the functions of all the senses, and of the life breath, as oblations into the fire of the controlled mind."

BG 5:11

"The yogis, abandoning attachment, act with body, mind, intelligence and even with the senses, only for the purpose of purification."

BG 15:7

"The living entities in this conditioned world are My eternal fragmental parts. Due to conditioned life, they are struggling very hard with the six senses, which include the mind."

B is for

Bal Gopal

Little boy Krishna

Worship of the deity as a child allows us to develop a loving relationship with Krishna.

BG 9:22

"But those who always worship Me with exclusive devotion, meditating on My transcendental form—to them I carry what they lack, and I preserve what they have."

C is for

Cows

That Krishna and the cowherd boys look after

Krishna and His friends cared for the cows in Vrindavan. We too have a natural love for all living beings.

BG 12:13–14

"One who is not envious but is a kind friend to all living entities, who does not think himself a proprietor and is free from false ego, who is equal in both happiness and distress, who is tolerant, always satisfied, self-controlled, and engaged in devotional service with determination, his mind and intelligence fixed on Me—such a devotee of Mine is very dear to Me."

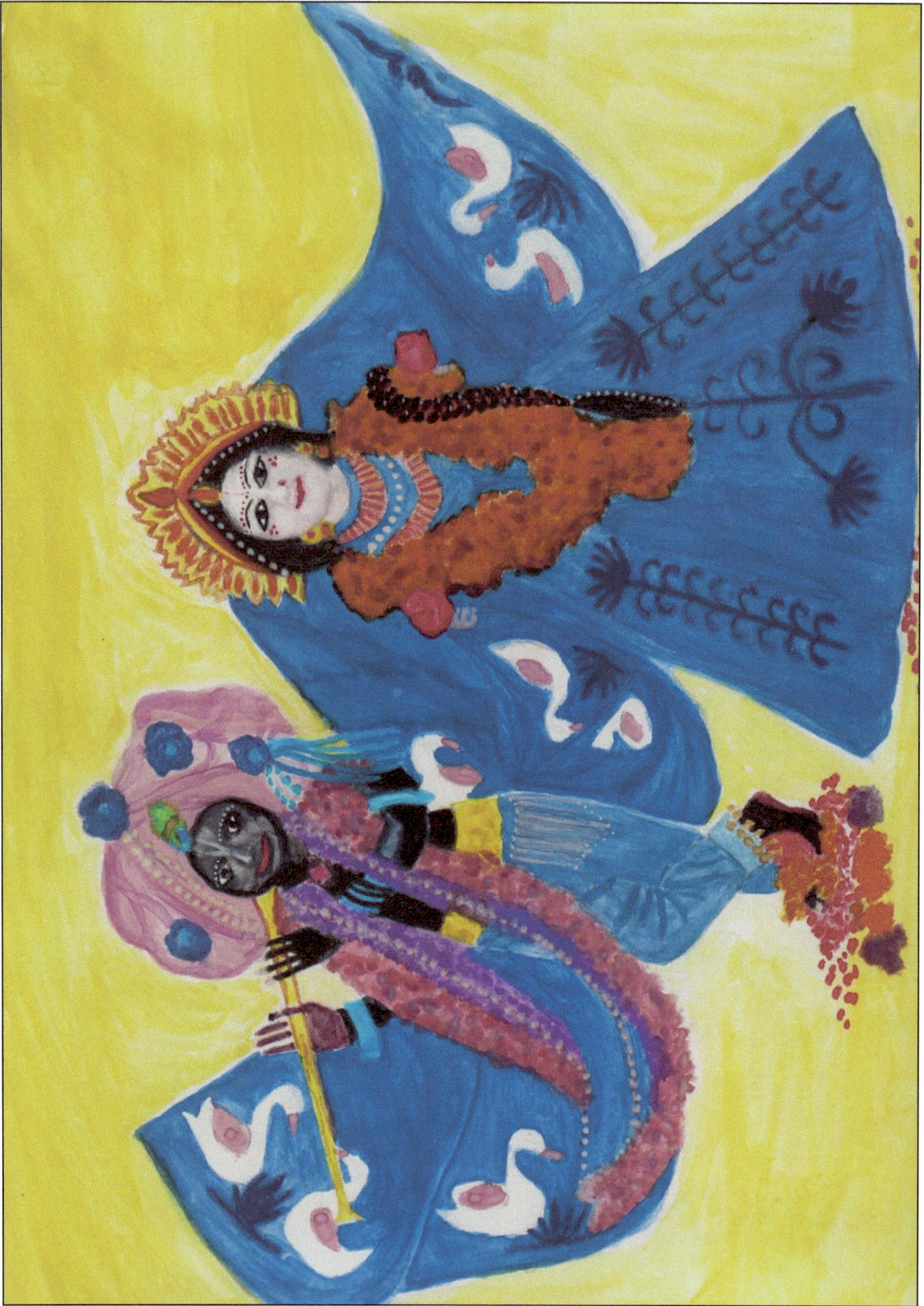

D is for

Deity

Krishna is so kind as to let us worship Him as our Deity

Worship develops our loving relationship with Krishna.

BG 12:2

"The Supreme Personality of Godhead said: Those who fix their minds on My personal form and are always engaged in worshiping Me with great and transcendental faith are considered by Me to be most perfect."

CC Madhya 20.108–109

"It is the living entity's constitutional position to be an eternal servant of Kṛṣṇa because he is the marginal energy of Kṛṣṇa and a manifestation simultaneously one with and different from the Lord, like a molecular particle of sunshine or fire. Kṛṣṇa has three varieties of energy."

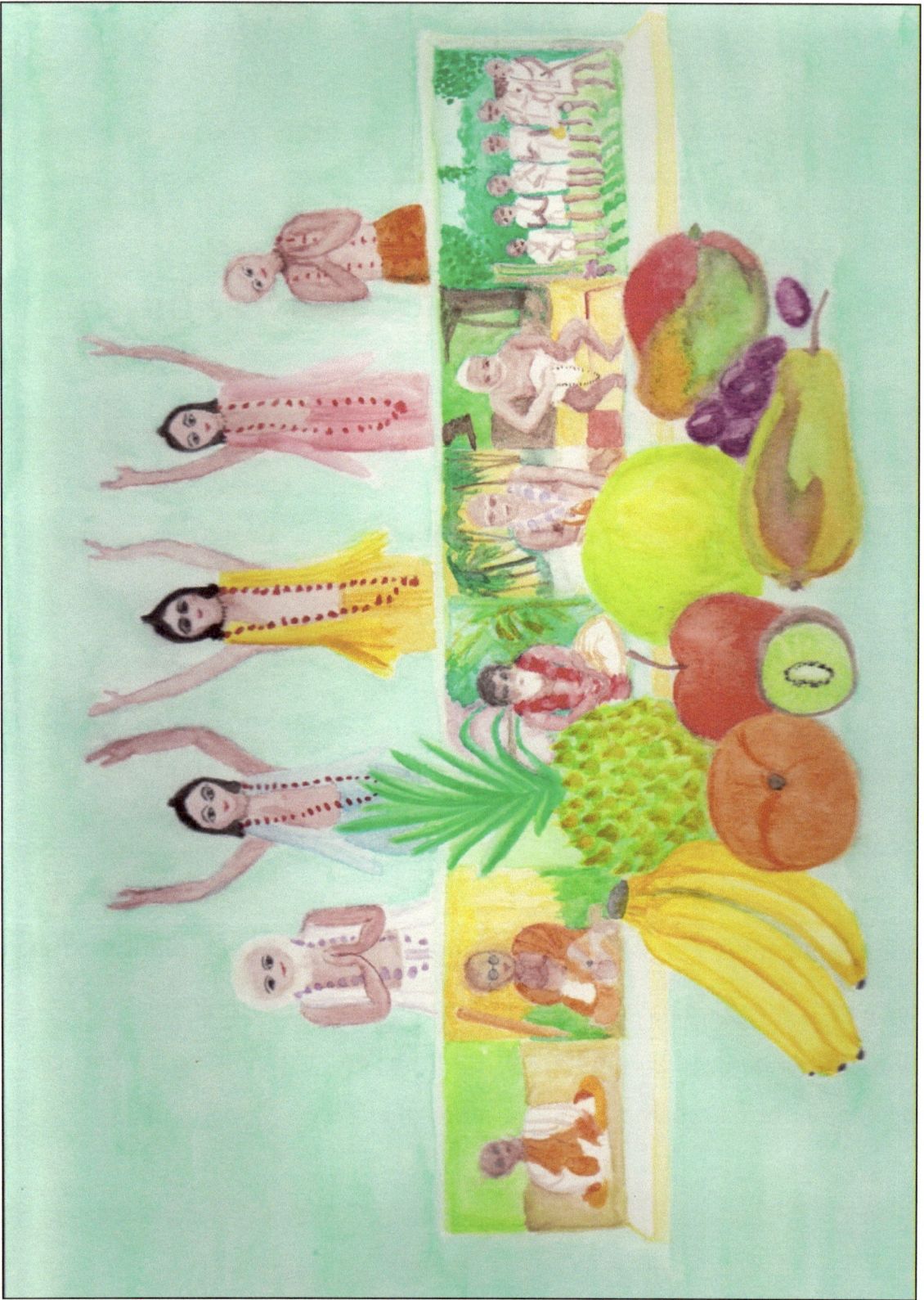

E is for

Ekadashi

The day we eat delicious vegetables, fruit and dairy offered to Krishna

By eating food offered first to Krishna (*prasadam*) we purify ourselves. Krishna is the owner and controller of everything. Thus, by offering food to Krishna, we recognise that we are dependent on Krishna.

BG 2:59

"Though the embodied soul may be restricted from sense enjoyment, the taste for sense objects remains. But, ceasing such engagements by experiencing a higher taste, he is fixed in consciousness."

BG 3:13

"The devotees of the Lord are released from all kinds of sins because they eat food which is offered first for sacrifice. Others, who prepare food for personal sense enjoyment, verily eat only sin."

F is for

Flute

That touches Krishna's lips

The sound vibration from Krishna's flute calls us back to Him.

KB 21: The Gopīs Attracted by the Flute

"Kṛṣṇa was very expert in playing the flute, and the *gopīs* were captivated by the sound vibration, which was attractive not only to them but to all living creatures who heard it. One of the *gopīs* told her friends, 'The highest perfection of the eyes is to see Kṛṣṇa and Balarāma entering the forest and playing Their flutes and tending the cows with Their friends.'"

G is for

Govardan Hill

Where Krishna played with His cowherd friends and looked after the cows

Govardhan Hill is adjacent to the city of Vrindavan, where Krishna lived 5,000 years ago.

BG 8:22

"The Supreme Personality of Godhead, who is greater than all, is attainable by unalloyed devotion. Although He is present in His abode, He is all-pervading, and everything is situated within Him."

BG 18:55–57

"One can understand Me as I am, as the Supreme Personality of Godhead, only by devotional service. And when one is in full consciousness of Me by such devotion, he can enter into the kingdom of God.

"Though engaged in all kinds of activities, My pure devotee, under My protection, reaches the eternal and imperishable abode by My grace.

"In all activities just depend upon Me and work always under My protection. In such devotional service, be fully conscious of Me."

H is for

Harinam Sankirtan

Singing of Krishna's name for all to hear

Singing Krishna's names (*kirtan*) is a lot of fun. Perhaps, you have gone to a Ratha Yatra parade and taken Jagannath, Baladeva and Subdhra out of the temple for a ride on the *yatra* cart.

BG 9:2

"This knowledge is the king of education, the most secret of all secrets. It is the purest knowledge, and because it gives direct perception of the self by realization, it is the perfection of religion. It is everlasting, and it is joyfully performed."

I is for

Indra

King of the gods, who offers his prayers to Krishna

In *Krishna Book*, the story of Indra, the King of the gods, is told. Indra was angry that sacrifices were not offered to him and he caused a storm to flood Vrindavan. Krishna saved all the people and animals of Vrindavan by lifting Govardhan Hill above His head on the little finger of His left hand to provide shelter.

SB 10.27.15

"The Supreme Personality of Godhead said: My dear Indra, it was out of mercy that I stopped the sacrifice meant for you. You were greatly intoxicated by your opulence as King of heaven, and I wanted you to always remember Me."

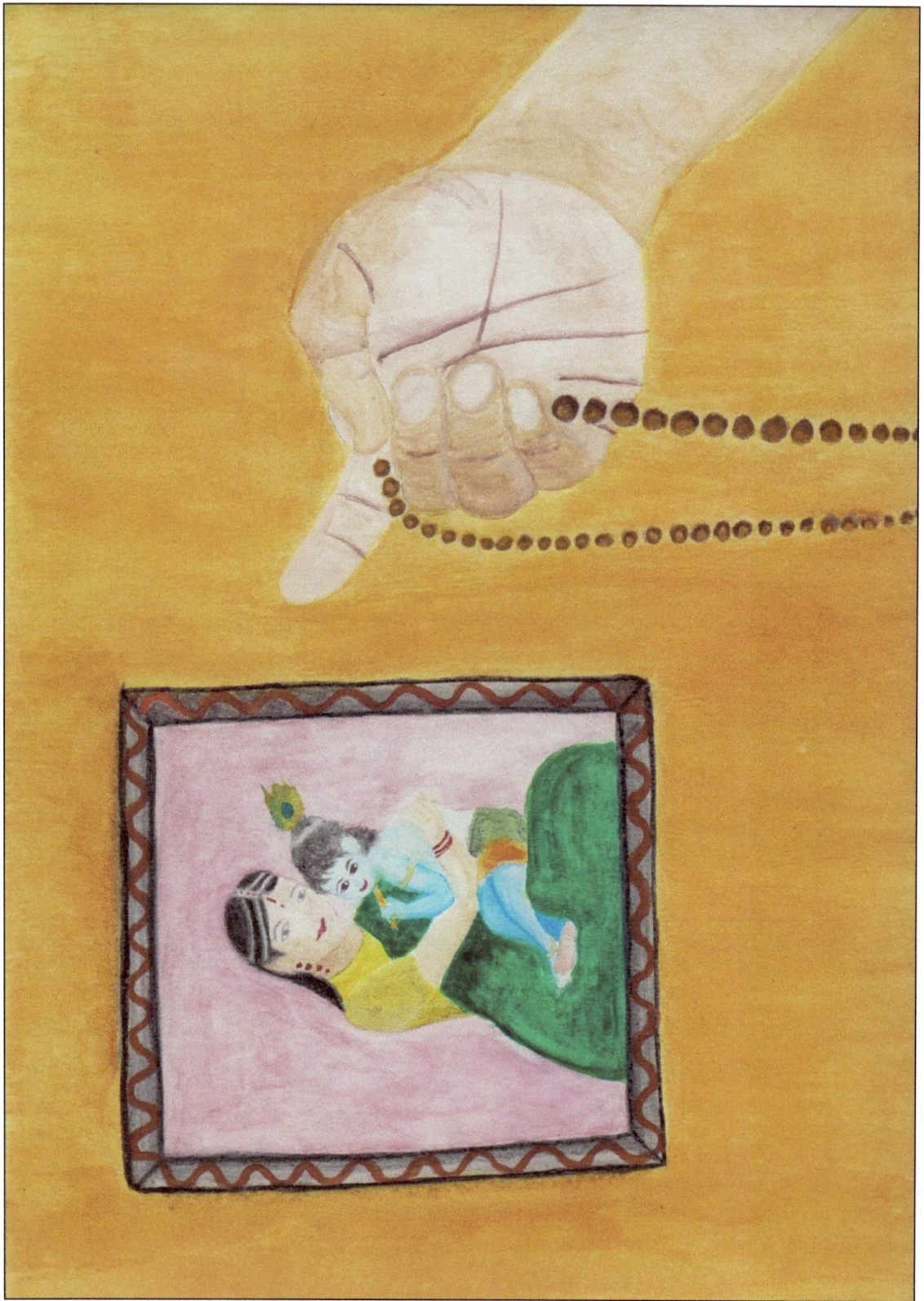

J is for

Japa beads

Used to count the maha mantra:

"Hare Krishna, Hare Krishna, Krishna, Krishna, Hare, Hare, Hare Rama, Hare Rama, Rama, Rama, Hare, Hare"

Chanting the maha mantra on a string of 108 beads, while thinking of Krishna, is purifying.

BG: 9:14

"Always chanting My glories, endeavoring with great determination, bowing down before Me, these great souls perpetually worship Me with devotion."

BG 10:25

"Of the great sages I am Bhṛgu; of vibrations I am the transcendental oṁ. Of sacrifices I am the chanting of the holy names [japa], and of immovable things I am the Himālayas."

K is for

Krishna

Our closest friend

Krishna is our best friend and well wisher. He guides us, if we only listen.

BG: 9:18

"I am the goal, the sustainer, the master, the witness, the abode, the refuge and the most dear friend. I am the creation and the annihilation, the basis of everything, the resting place and the eternal seed."

BG 9:29

"I envy no one, nor am I partial to anyone. I am equal to all. But whoever renders service unto Me in devotion is a friend, is in Me, and I am also a friend to him."

L is for

Lotus

Flowers which have soft petals like Krishna's feet and petals shaped like Krishna's eyes

Krishna carries a lotus in His hand.

BG 5:10

"One who performs his duty without attachment, surrendering the results unto the Supreme God, is not affected by sinful action, as the lotus leaf is untouched by water."

M is for

Mridanga

The drum that keeps the beat to songs sung for Krishna

Singing and listening to songs about Krishna is a lot of fun. Have you listened and sung with others in the temple or at the Ratha Yatra?

BG 7:17

"Of these, the one who is in full knowledge and who is always engaged in pure devotional service is the best. For I am very dear to him, and he is dear to Me."

N is for

Narasimha

Krishna in the form of half lion, half man who came to protect his devotee Pralad

Krishna is most powerful, and always protects His devotee. Pralad was a young devotee of Krishna. His stories are described in *Transcendental Teachings of Prahlāda Mahārāja*.

BG 9:30–31

"Even if one commits the most abominable action, if he is engaged in devotional service, he is to be considered saintly because he is properly situated in his determination.

"He quickly becomes righteous and attains lasting peace. O son of Kunti, declare it boldly that My devotee never perishes."

O is for

Obeisance

We bow down in obeisance to Krishna

Bowing to the spiritual master and the deity develops our loving relationship with Krishna.

BG 9:34

"Engage your mind always in thinking of Me, become My devotee, offer obeisances to Me and worship Me. Being completely absorbed in Me, surely you will come to Me."

P is for

Prabhupada

Who taught the world about Krishna

Srila Prabhupada came to the western world from India to teach about Krishna on the request of his spiritual master in 1966. He started the Hare Krishna movement by sharing the profound teachings of *The Bhagavad Gita*, *Srimad Bhagvatam* and *Chaitanya Charitamrita*.

BG 4:34

"Just try to learn the truth by approaching a spiritual master. Inquire from him submissively and render service unto him. The self-realized soul can impart knowledge unto you because he has seen the truth."

BG 18:68–70

"For one who explains this supreme secret to the devotees, pure devotional service is guaranteed, and at the end he will come back to Me.

"There is no servant in this world more dear to Me than he, nor will there ever be one more dear.

"And I declare that he who studies this sacred conversation of ours worships Me by his intelligence."

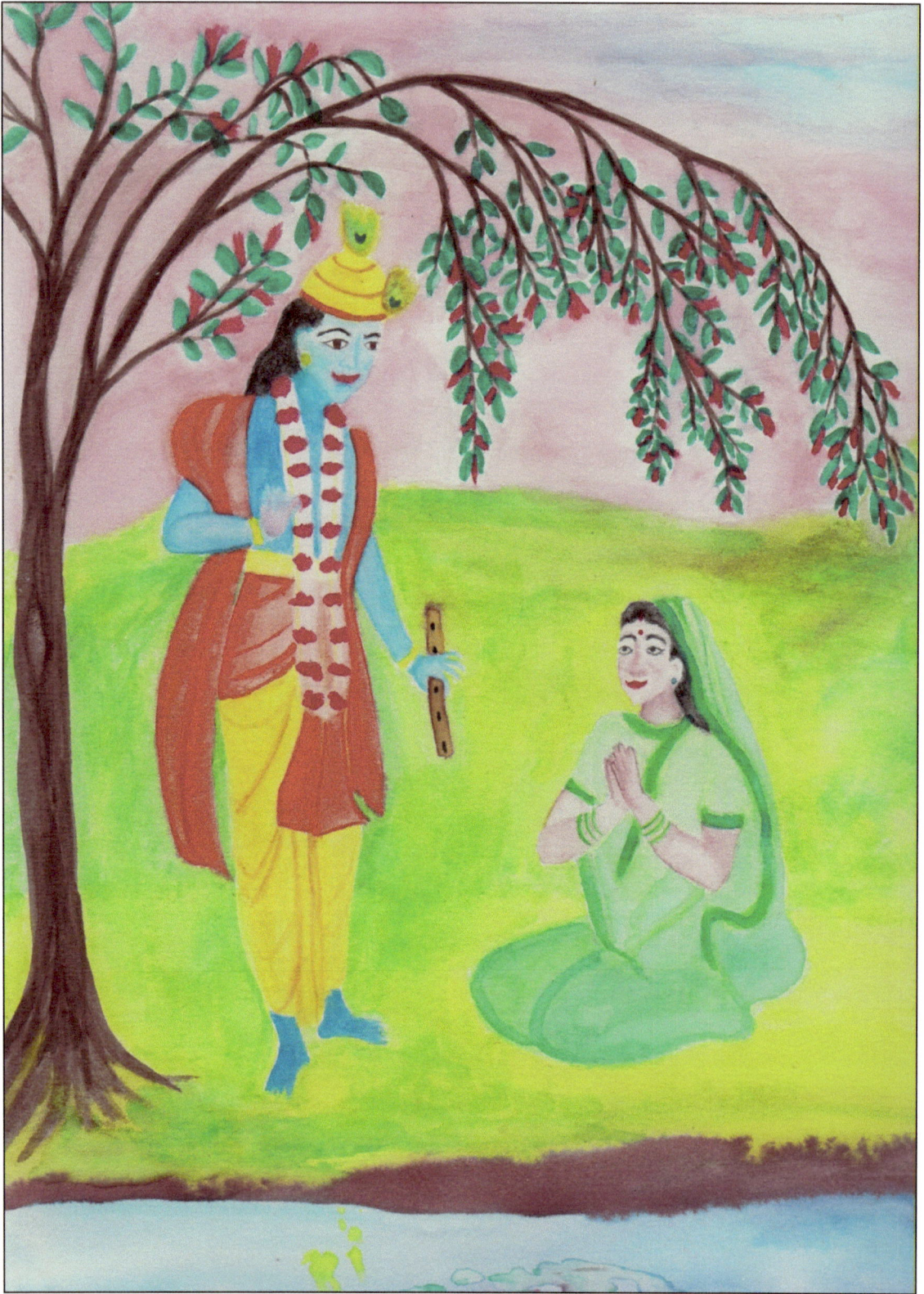

Q is for

Queen Kunti

The aunt of Krishna (Krishna's father's sister)

Queen Kunti prayed for calamities so that she could always remember Krishna. Remembering Krishna is the devotee's goal.

Śrīmad Bhāgavatam 1.8.25

"I wish that all those calamities would happen again and again so that we could see You again and again, for seeing You means that we will no longer see repeated births and deaths."

R is for

Radha

Krishna's most dear childhood friend

Radha was Krishna's friend in Vrindavan. When Krishna left Vrindavan to fight demons, She lived by remembering Krishna always.

BG 6:30

"For one who sees Me everywhere and sees everything in Me, I am never lost, nor is he ever lost to Me."

S is for

Satsang

Gathering together to talk about Krishna and Krishna's pastimes

Talking about Krishna and His pastimes (*Krishna katha*) with other devotees is blissful.

BG 10:9–11

"The thoughts of My pure devotees dwell in Me, their lives are fully devoted to My service, and they derive great satisfaction and bliss from always enlightening one another and conversing about Me.

"To those who are constantly devoted and worship Me with love, I give the understanding by which they can come to Me.

"To show them special mercy, I, dwelling in their hearts, destroy with the shining lamp of knowledge the darkness born of ignorance."

T is for

Tulsi

One of Krishna's favorite plants

Do you grow tulsi plants in your house or garden? Tulsi leaves are offered to Krishna by placing them on His feet.

BG 18:65

"Always think of Me and become My devotee. Worship Me and offer your homage unto Me. Thus you will come to Me without fail. I promise you this because you are My very dear friend."

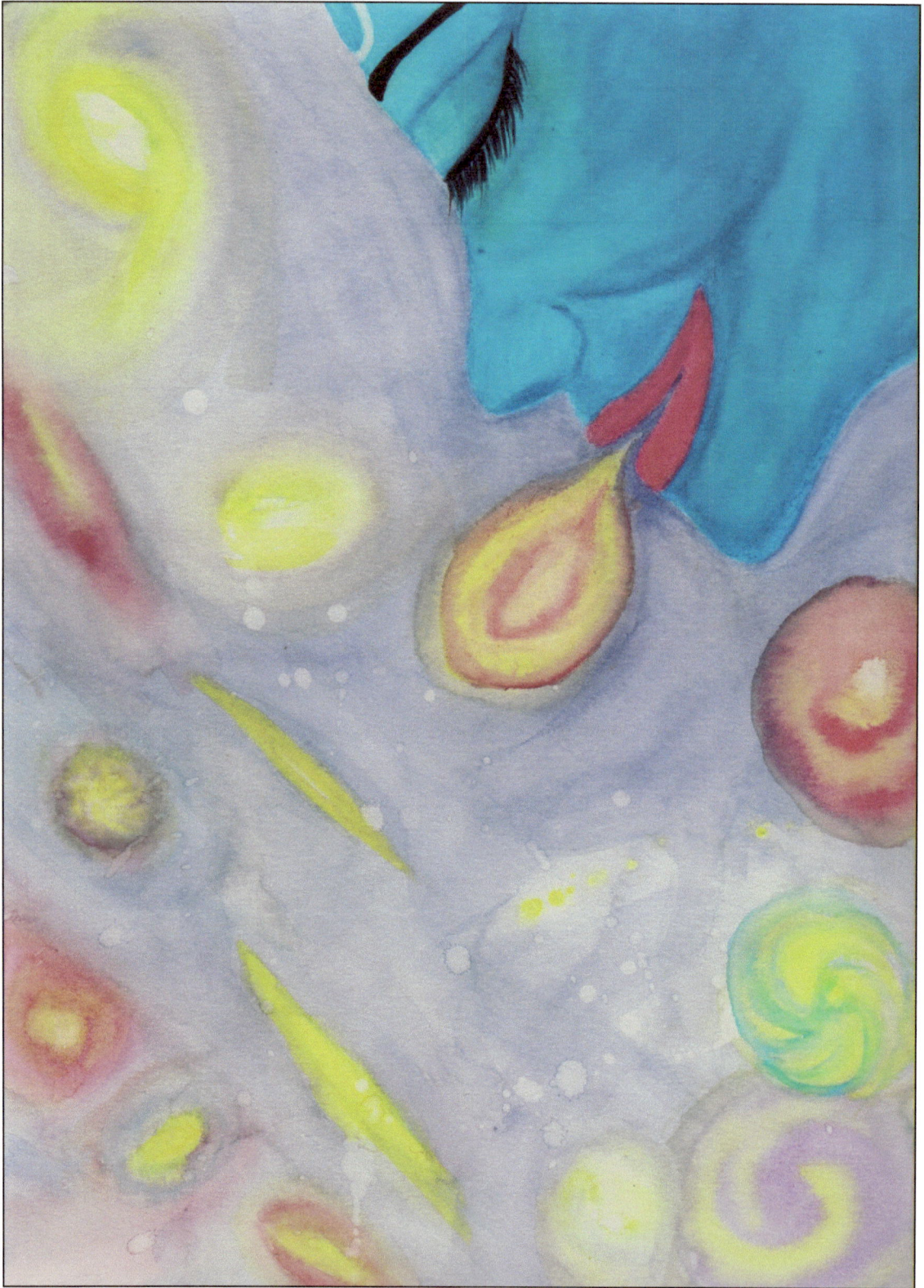

U is for

Universes

Breathed out from the pores of Mahavishnu (Krishna)

Looking up at the sky and seeing so many stars makes us realize how small we are, and how small our problems are in comparison to the cosmic creation. Have you ever seen a solar or lunar eclipse, or gone to the planetarium?

BG 8:9

"One should meditate upon the Supreme Person as the one who knows everything, as He who is the oldest, who is the controller, who is smaller than the smallest, who is the maintainer of everything, who is beyond all material conception, who is inconceivable, and who is always a person. He is luminous like the sun, and He is transcendental, beyond this material nature."

BG 10:8

"I am the source of all spiritual and material worlds. Everything emanates from Me. The wise who perfectly know this engage in My devotional service and worship Me with all their hearts."

V is for

Vrindavana

Where Krishna lived as a boy

Vrindavan is the eternal home of Krishna, and we can go there in our imagination. Have you ever closed your eyes and thought of a place or person and felt that you could see them?

BG 8:28

"A person who accepts the path of devotional service is not bereft of the results derived from studying the Vedas, performing sacrifices, undergoing austerities, giving charity or pursuing philosophical and fruitive activities. Simply by performing devotional service, he attains all these, and at the end he reaches the supreme eternal abode."

W is for

Water

Offered to Krishna

Water is thirst quenching like no other drink. Have you noticed that when you are thirsty, water is the best drink? Since Krishna is the taste of water, you can remember Him when you take a drink of water.

BG 7:8

"O son of Kunti, I am the taste of water, the light of the sun and the moon, the syllable om in the Vedic mantras; I am the sound in ether and the ability in man."

X is for

Xylophone

Used to make music for Krishna

Xylophones or any other musical instrument can be used to make music and sing for Krishna. Have you participated in a *kirtan*?

BG 11:54–55

"My dear Arjuna, only by undivided devotional service can I be understood as I am, standing before you, and can thus be seen directly. Only in this way can you enter into the mysteries of My understanding.

"My dear Arjuna, he who engages in My pure devotional service, free from the contaminations of fruitive activities and mental speculation, he who works for Me, who makes Me the supreme goal of his life, and who is friendly to every living being—he certainly comes to Me."

Y is for

Yamuna

The river that flows through Vrindavan where Krishna grew up

Have you sailed in a boat on a river? Some rivers are small and fast flowing and others are wide and deep.

BG 2:70

"A person who is not disturbed by the incessant flow of desires—that enter like rivers into the ocean, which is ever being filled but is always still—can alone achieve peace, and not the man who strives to satisfy such desires."

Z is for

Zinnia

Flowers that make a garland for Krishna

Have you made a garland for Krishna? Do you have a garden? You can offer flowers to Krishna.

BG 9:26–28

"If one offers Me with love and devotion a leaf, a flower, a fruit or water, I will accept it.

"Whatever you do, whatever you eat, whatever you offer or give away, and whatever austerities you perform—do that, O son of Kunti, as an offering unto Me.

"In this way you will be freed from bondage to work and its auspicious and inauspicious results. With your mind fixed on Me in this principle of renunciation, you will be liberated and come to Me."

Glossary

Arati: Worship by offering lamps, flowers, water, or incense to God

Bal: A little boy

Gopal: One who looks after cows

Ekadashi: A day every two weeks (based on the phase of the moon) when devotees of Krishna fast from grains

Gobardhan: A hill near Vrindavana in India

Harinam: *Hari* (another name of Krishna) *nam* (name), or Krishna's name

Japa: The repetition of a chant counted on beads as a form of meditation

Katha: Story

Mridanga: A long drum with two sides to beat on

Narasimha: *Nara* (man) *simha* (lion), or Krishna in the form of half man, half lion

Sankirtan: Songs of praise and devotion to Lord Krishna

Tulsi: A plant of the basil family

Vrindavana: A town in India where Krishna grew up approximately 5,000 years ago

Yamuna: A river that flows through the town of Vrindavana

www.ingramcontent.com/pod-product-compliance
Lightning Source LLC
LaVergne TN
LVHW072113070426
835510LV00002B/26